I SING A SONG
OF THE
SAINTS
OF GOD

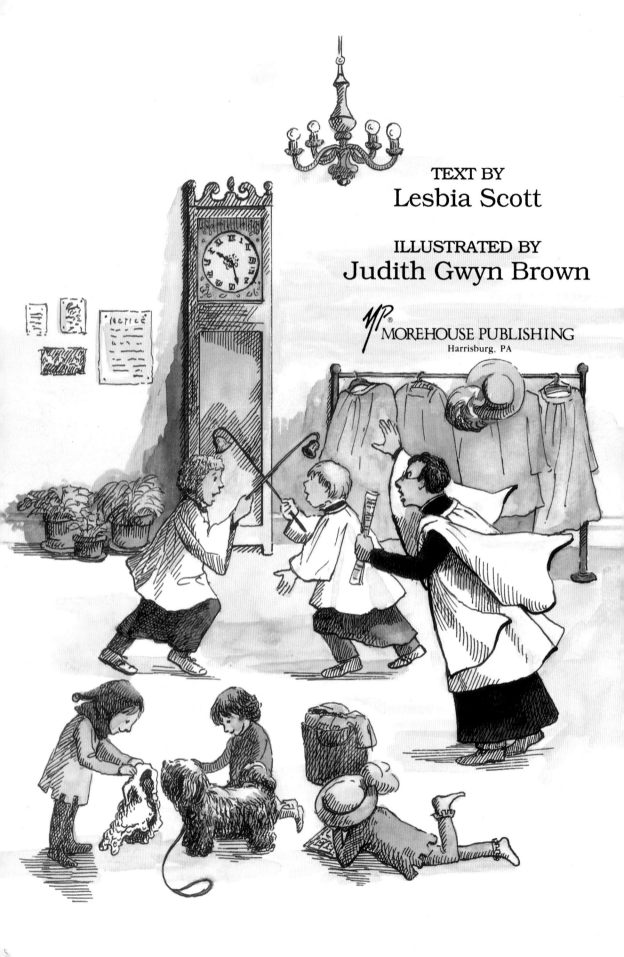

TEXT BY
Lesbia Scott

ILLUSTRATED BY
Judith Gwyn Brown

MOREHOUSE PUBLISHING
Harrisburg, PA

I SING A SONG OF THE
SAINTS OF GOD

Text © 1929 by Lesbia Scott. Used by permission of Morehouse Publishing.

Illustrations © 1981 Judith Gwyn Brown

Morehouse Publishing

Editorial Office:
871 Ethan Allen Highway
Suite 204
Ridgefield, CT 06877

Corporate Office:
P.O. Box 1321
Harrisburg, PA 17105

Library of Congress Cataloging-in-Publication Data

Scott, Lesbia.
    I sing a song of the saints of God/illustrated by Judith Gwyn Brown; [text by Lesbia Scott].
        p.   cm.
    Summary: A page of music is included for this hymn praising the saints who have gone before us and those we meet in our daily lives. Also includes brief biographies of six saints.
    ISBN 0-8192-1618-6
    1. Hymns, English—Juvenile literature. 2. Christian saints—Juvenile literature. 3. Communion of saints—Juvenile literature. [1. Hymns. 2. Saints.] I. Brown, Judith Gwyn ill. II. Title.
[BV353.S38   1991]   91-10393
264'.2—dc20   CIP
                                                                AC MN

Printed in Malaysia
Third printing in paper, 1997

This book is dedicated to
Herbert G. Draesel, Jr.
Rector
The Church of the Holy Trinity, New York, N.Y.
and
To the rebuilt Church of
St. Luke-in-the-Fields,
Greenwich Village, New York.

Heaven and earth are as a musical instrument;
if you touch a string below, the motion goes
to the top. Any good done to Christ's poor
members upon earth affects him in heaven.
John Donne
(1573 - 1631)

I sing a song of the saints of God . . .
Patient and brave and true,

Who toiled and fought and lived and died
For the Lord they loved and knew.

And one was a doctor,

ST. MARGARET

and one was a queen,

and one was a shepherdess on the green:

They were all of them saints of God—
    and I mean,
God helping, to be one too.

They loved their Lord so dear, so dear,
    And his love made them strong;
And they followed the right, for Jesus' sake,
    The whole of their good lives long.

And one was a soldier,

and one was a priest,

JOHN
DONNE
PRIEST

and one was slain by a fierce wild beast:

And there's not any reason—
    no, not the least—
Why I shouldn't be one too.

They lived not only in ages past,
    There are hundreds of thousands still,

The world is bright with joyous saints
Who love to do Jesus' will.

You can meet them in school, or in lanes,

or at sea,

In church, or in trains, or in shops,

or at tea,

For the saints of God

are just folk

like me,

And I mean to be one too.

I SING A SONG OF THE

Text by Lesbia Scott, 1929 (alt.)
Tune: Grand Isle, John Henry Hopkins, 1940
Harmonized by William F. Entriken, 1981
Hymn used by permission of Morehouse Publishing.

SAINTS of GOD

1

I sing a song of the saints of God
  Patient and brave and true,
Who toiled and fought and lived and died
  For the Lord they loved and knew.
    And one was a doctor, and one was a queen,
    And one was a shepherdess on the green:
    They were all of them saints of God—and I mean,
    God helping, to be one too.

2

They loved their Lord so dear, so dear,
  And his love made them strong;
And they followed the right, for Jesus' sake,
  The whole of their good lives long.
    And one was a soldier, and one was a priest,
    And one was slain by a fierce wild beast:
    And there's not any reason—no, not the least—
    Why I shouldn't be one too.

3

They lived not only in ages past,
  There are hundreds of thousands still,
The world is bright with joyous saints
  Who love to do Jesus' will.
    You can meet them in school, or in lanes, or at sea,
    In church, or in trains, or in shops, or at tea,
    For the saints of God are just folk like me,
    And I mean to be one too.

THE SAINTS WE SING ABOUT

A Doctor

LUKE, who was born in Antioch, in Syria, in the first century of the modern era, was a man of many talents. He was a writer (he wrote the Gospel that is named for him, and the Acts of the Apostles), a physician, and a painter (according to some people). Luke is the patron saint of physicians and surgeons, and of painters, too. The "Beloved Physician," as Luke was called, is remembered on October 18—and every other day we hear his words in scripture. His symbol is a winged ox.

A Queen

MARGARET OF SCOTLAND, who was really born in Hungary around 1045, was brought to Britain by her parents as a young girl. She grew up and married King Malcolm III of Scotland in 1070. They had eight children—six sons and two daughters. Margaret was a religious woman and *determined* as well. She was *determined* to be a good mother (she was), determined to be a good influence on the manners of the Scots (she may have been), and determined to help orphans and poor people as much as she could (she did). She died in Edinburgh in 1093. She is remembered on November 16. Her son David also became known as a saint—and as one of the best kings Scotland ever had.

A Shepherdess on the Green

JOAN OF ARC, who was also called "the Maid of Orleans," was born in France—at Domremy in the province of Champagne—around 1412. Joan lived in the country and probably herded sheep and worked in the orchards and fields like the other children. But from the time she was thirteen, Joan felt she had a special calling from the Lord to help save her country from its enemies; in fact, she heard voices, heavenly voices, that told her she would be called to act more courageously than any other person in Domremy, in Champagne, or even in France. In 1429, when she was barely seventeen years old, Joan was able to convince the Dauphin, the crown prince of France, that she must ride with him into battle against his enemies—the English and the rebellious Burgundians. When the prince and his advisors were convinced of Joan's goodness and sincerity, she did indeed ride into battle beside her prince and in full armor. She helped win many victories, but she was captured by her enemies in 1430. The brave young woman was put to death in 1431. Although many people in France and elsewhere believed that Joan was a saint—even while she was still alive—she was not proclaimed one until 1920. She is remembered on May 30, and on every other day her story is told and her courage and faithfulness to God's will are recalled.

A Soldier

MARTIN OF TOURS was the son of a soldier. He was born in Hungary where his father was serving around AD 315, but he was brought up in Italy. He followed his family tradition and became a soldier like his father. One day, when serving at Amiens, in France, Martin was out riding his horse. As he rode he spotted a poor, shivering, naked beggar standing in the dust. Martin reined in his horse, dismounted, tore his fine cloak in half, and gave half to the beggar so he could warm himself. Martin did this because he felt sorry for the beggar, but also because he saw the face of Christ in the beggar's face. When he was about twenty-four, Martin decided it was time to leave the army. "I am Christ's soldier," he said, "I am not allowed to fight." Many of his former comrades thought that Martin was a coward—but he knew better. He became a priest and was eventually made bishop of Tours. He founded many monasteries and served God wherever he went throughout a good, long life. Martin was so anxious to bring the Word of God to all parts of his diocese that he travelled constantly—on foot, by water, and even on donkey-back. He died near Tours in 397. His life and bravery are remembered on November 11.

A Priest

JOHN DONNE was born in London in 1573. He does not have a "ST" before his name, but he was surely a saint of God. He was first a writer, a poet who wrote with great skill and beauty. But in 1614 he was urged by his king, James I, to become an Anglican priest: he took the king's suggestion. Eventually he was elected dean of London's famous cathedral church of St. Paul, and he also won fame throughout England as a fine preacher who spoke the Word of God with great skill. John Donne was a man who devoted his talents, which were many, to the glory of God. He died in 1631, and he is remembered whenever one of his poems or sermons is read.

Slain by a Fierce Wild Beast

IGNATIUS OF ANTIOCH was probably born in Syria. He was eventually bishop of the great Christian community at Antioch. He lived so long ago that we are not sure when he was born; but we know he died a hero's death around AD 115. He was a good letter writer and wrote to his Christian followers of his love for them and for God. But the Romans who ruled much of the world in those days were determined to wipe out Christianity if they could. When Ignatius was an old man the Roman officials in Antioch seized him and condemned him to death. He was sent back to Rome to be thrown to fierce wild beasts in the Colosseum. Ignatius was not afraid. In fact, he is said to have remarked, on hearing of his cruel death sentence, "Let me follow the example of the suffering of my God." He is remembered on October 17.

AND ALL THE REST WHO LOVE TO DO JESUS' WILL, which may mean the policeman on the corner, or your grandmother, or the teacher in school (yes, it is possible), or your best friend—or even YOU.